Kids' Travel Guide
France & Paris

FlyingKids Presents:
Kids' Travel Guide
France & Paris

Writer: **Shira Halperin**

Editor: **Yael Ornan**

Designer: Keren **Amram**, Slavisa **Zivkovic**

Cover Designer: Francesca Guido

Illustrator: **Liat Aluf**

Translator: Oren Amir

Translation editor: Carma Graber

Published by FlyingKids Limited

Visit us: www.theflyingkids.com

Contact us: leonardo@theflyingkids.com

ISBN: 978-1-910994-06-1

Acknowledgements: All images are from FlyingKids or public domain except those mentioned below. Shutterstock images: pp. 10, 15, 27, 29, 32, 33, 37, 41, 44, 46, 47, 48, 51, 58, & 59; Dollar Photo Club: PP. 11, 16, 35.

Table of Contents

Dear Parents,

If you bought this book, you're probably planning a family trip with your kids. You are spending a lot of time and money in the hopes that this family vacation will be pleasant and fun. Of course, you would like your children to get to know the place you are visiting — a little of its geography, local history, important sites, culture, customs, and more. And you hope they will always remember the trip as a very special experience.

The reality is often quite different. Parents find themselves frustrated as they struggle to convince their kids to join a tour or visit a landmark, while the kids just want to stay in and watch TV. Or the kids are glued to their mobile devices and don't pay much attention to the new sights and places of interest. Many parents are disappointed when they return home and discover that their kids don't remember much about the trip and the new things they learned.

That's exactly why the Kids' Travel Guide series was created.

With the Kids' Travel Guides, young children become researchers and active participants in the trip. During the vacation, kids will read relevant facts about the place you are visiting. The Kids' Travel Guides include puzzles, tasks to complete, useful tips, and other recommendations along the way.

The kids will meet Leonardo — their tour guide. Leonardo encourages them to experiment, explore, and be more involved in the family's activities — as well as to learn new information and make memories throughout the trip. In addition, kids are encouraged to document and write about their experiences during the trip, so that when you return home, they will have a memoir that will be fun to look at and reread again and again.

The Kids' Travel Guides support children as they get ready for the trip, visit new places, learn new things, and finally, return home.

The *Kids' Travel Guide — France & Paris* focuses on France and the City of Light — Paris. In it, children will learn about France — its geography, history, unique culture, traditions, and more — along with background information on Paris and its special attractions. The Paris portion of the book concentrates on central sites that are recommended for children. At each of these sites, interesting facts, action items, and quizzes await your kids. You, the parents, are invited to participate, or to find an available bench and relax while you enjoy your active children.

Have a great Family Trip!

Hi, Kids!

If you are reading this book, it means you are lucky — you aree going to Paris, France!

You may have noticed that your parents are getting ready for the journey. They have bought travel guides, looked for information on the Internet, and printed pages of information. They are talking to friends and people who have already visited France and Paris, in order to learn about it and know what to do, where to go, and when ... But this is not just another guidebook for your parents. This book is for you only — the young traveler.

So what is this book all about?

First and foremost, meet **Leonardo**, your very own personal guide on this trip. Leonardo has visited many places around the world. (Guess how he got there?) He will be with you throughout the book and the trip.

Leonardo will tell you all about the places you will visit ...

It is always good to learn a little about the country and city you are visiting and its history beforehand. Leonardo will give you many ideas, quizzes, tips, and other surprises. He will accompany you while you are packing and leaving home. He will stay in the hotel with you (don't worry — it doesn't cost more money)! And he will see the sights with you until you return home.

A Travel Diary —The Beginning!
Going to France & Paris!!!

How did you get to France?

By plane / train / car / other _____

Date of arrival _____ Time _____ Date of departure _____

All in all, we will stay in Paris for _____ days.

Is this your first visit _____ ?

Where will you sleep? hotel / campsite / apartment / with family / other _____

What sites are you planning on visiting?

_____

_____

_____

What special activities are you planning on doing?

_____

_____

_____

Are you excited about the trip?

This is an excitement indicator. Ask each family member how excited he or she is (from "not at all" up to "very, very much"), and mark it down on the indicator. Leonardo has also marked the level of his excitement…

not at all

very,
very much

Leonardo

Who is traveling?

Write down the names of family members traveling with you.

Name: _____

Age: _____

Has he or she visited France or Paris before? yes / no

What is the most exciting thing about your upcoming trip?

_____

_____

_____

Name: _____

Age: _____

Has he or she visited France or Paris before? yes / no

What is the most exciting thing about your upcoming trip?

_____

_____

Name: _____

Age: _____

Has he or she visited France or Paris before? yes / no

What is the most exciting thing about your upcoming trip?

_____

_____

Name: _____

Age: _____

Has he or she visited France or Paris before? yes / no

What is the most exciting thing about your upcoming trip?

_____

_____

Name: _____

Age: _____

Has he or she visited France or Paris before? yes / no

What is the most exciting thing about your upcoming trip?

_____

_____

Name: _____

Age: _____

Has he or she visited France or Paris before? yes / no

What is the most exciting thing about your upcoming trip?

_____

_____

Paste a picture of the
whole family here.

Preparations at home – do not forget...!

Mom or Dad will take care of packing clothes (how many pairs of pants, which comb to take...). Leonardo will only tell you about the stuff he thinks you may want to take along to France and Paris.

Here's the Packing List Leonardo made for you. You can check off each item as you pack it:

- *Kids' Travel Guide — France & Paris* — of course!
- Comfortable walking shoes
- A raincoat (One that folds up is best — sometimes it rains without warning ...)
- A hat (and sunglasses, if you want)
- Pens and pencils
- Crayons and markers (It is always nice to color and paint.)
- A notebook or writing pad (You can use it for games or writing, or to draw or doodle in when you're bored ...)
- A book to read
- Your smartphone/tablet or camera

Tips!

Pack a few things for the flight in a small bag (or backpack), such as:

- snacks, fruit, candy, and chewing gum. It may help a lot during takeoff and landing, when there's pressure in your ears.
- games you can play while sitting down: electronic games, booklets of crossword puzzles, connect-the-numbers (or connect-the-dots), etc.

Now let's see if you can find 12 items you should take on a trip in this word search puzzle:

P	A	T	I	E	N	C	E	A	W	F	G
E	L	R	T	S	G	Y	J	W	A	T	O
Q	E	Y	U	Y	K	Z	K	M	L	W	O
H	O	S	N	A	S	N	Y	S	K	G	D
A	N	R	Z	C	P	E	N	C	I	L	M
C	A	M	E	R	A	A	W	G	N	E	O
R	R	A	I	N	C	O	A	T	G	Q	O
Y	D	S	G	I	R	K	Z	K	S	H	D
S	O	A	C	O	A	E	T	K	H	A	T
F	R	U	I	T	Y	Q	O	V	O	D	A
B	O	O	K	F	O	H	Z	K	E	R	T
T	K	Z	K	A	N	S	I	E	S	Y	U
O	V	I	E	S	S	N	A	C	K	S	P

Leonardo, walking shoes, hat, raincoat, crayons, book, pencil, camera, snacks, fruit, patience, good mood

La France

France is one of the most beautiful countries in the world, and millions of people arrive there every year to enjoy its wonders: a rich **culture**, a fascinating history, **lovely cities**, great beaches, splendid **lakes**, exciting **ski** resorts, and **excellent food**.

Who knows which continent France is on?

(Answer on the next page.)

**This is a map of Europe.
Can you point out France?**

Go over France's borders and mark them.

Is your home country on the map?

YES / NO

Where is France?

10

France on the map

You may have noticed that France is located in the western part of Europe.
France is the third largest country in Europe. Only Russia and Ukraine are bigger.

What is a compass rose?

A compass rose is a drawing that shows the directions: North-South-East-West. North is always at the top of the map, and from that you can figure out the other directions.

When going on field trips, you can use a compass. A compass rose is drawn on the face of the compass, and the needle always points North.
Knowing each direction helps you navigate and find out where places are — or how to get from one point to another.

Mark the three missing directions in the blank squares.

North

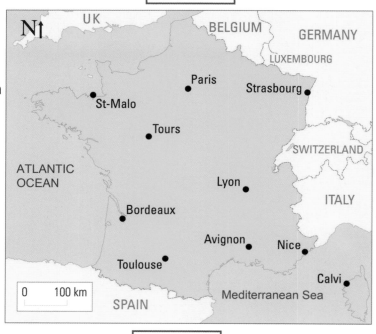

France is surrounded by many neighboring countries. Can you find them on the map? If so, complete the following:

To the South — _____

To the East — _____ , _____ , and _____

To the North — _____ and _____

Borders

Did you know?

In order to differentiate between countries, borders were invented. A border is a line that marks the end of one country's territory and the beginning of another. There are all kinds of borders; sometimes a river or a range of mountains are a natural border, or sometimes there is a fence or special gate to mark a border.

In France, for example, there's a natural border to the east: the French Alps, mountains that stretch between France, Italy, and Switzerland.

France is also surrounded by seas.
Can you find their names?

To the southeast _____

To the west _____

Quiz! What is the capital of France?

a. London

b. Elysees

c. Paris

Answer: c. Paris

d. The French Riviera

Answers: In the Southeast: The Mediterranean; In the West: The Atlantic Ocean

Do only French people live in France?

The majority of the people living in France are French (92 percent of its citizens), but there are also many immigrants* from North Africa and Germany.

*Immigrants are people who moved permanently to a country that is not their native country.

Do people in France speak French?

Of course! Most of the French people speak French, but if you listen carefully, you'll be able to hear other languages spoken as well. Most of these languages, such as Flemish, Alsatian, Breton, Basque, and Catalan, are not well-known.

Besides wonderful Paris, there are many other beautiful cities in France worth visiting.
Let's see if you can find **15 lovely French cities** in the following word search puzzle.

A	S	C	H	E	R	B	O	U	R	G	H	I	K	Z
M	F	H	T	J	K	N	T	O	U	L	U	O	S	E
A	V	U	A	S	A	G	Z	N	Q	E	R	V	N	B
R	E	I	O	K	Z	T	O	A	I	L	H	E	L	E
S	L	P	R	R	J	R	E	N	M	C	J	I	I	H
E	G	B	L	I	L	L	E	T	Q	E	E	W	M	N
I	R	Y	E	M	G	K	L	E	E	Y	T	U	O	G
L	E	P	A	R	I	S	W	S	C	S	D	K	G	B
L	N	I	N	O	G	D	N	T	X	H	I	N	E	O
E	O	K	S	U	G	V	V	K	C	B	J	V	S	R
A	B	P	O	E	F	X	T	W	Q	A	O	Z	F	D
Q	L	Y	O	N	I	B	R	E	S	T	N	J	T	E
D	E	E	B	N	K	L	P	S	X	C	B	Y	T	A
D	T	M	O	N	T	E	C	A	R	L	O	G	E	U
J	I	R	F	G	H	K	O	C	A	M	U	J	M	X

Paris, Monte Carlo, Bordeaux, Orleans, Rouen, Toulouse, Nice, Marseille, Nantes, Lille, Cherbourg, Lyon, Dijon, Brest, Limoges, Grenoble

What other beautiful tourist attractions and sites are there in France?

The French Alps' beauty is overwhelming. The region is rich with high mountains, valleys, and sparkling **lakes** and **rivers**. Its beauty attracts many tourists from all over the world. In winter, you can go **skiing** on the snowy mountain slopes, and in summer **enjoy the scenic drives in nature.**

What is a valley? A lowland surrounded by mountains or hills.

The French Riviera is a resort area, famous in France and worldwide. In French, the Riviera is called *La Côte D'Azure*, meaning "sky-blue coast." There are small resort villages in the Riviera, beautiful cities such as Marseille, Cannes, and Monaco, and naturally, some splendid and exotic beaches. It is said that the residents of this region are not at all like the typical French people; they are much more relaxed and calm (no wonder…). The rich and the famous love to spend time in the French Riviera, and you may be lucky enough to see a famous movie star driving by in a fancy car…

Flags, symbols, and coins

This is the **flag** of **France**.

The French call it *Le Tricolore*. If you don't know what 'tricolor" means, take a look at the flag and try to figure it out by counting the number of colors ("tri" means three) 😊.

Did you know?

In the past, each stripe was of a different width. It was Napoleon who decided that the stripes should all be the same size, and he changed the flag — although the French army still uses the old one.

This is the symbol of France. If you take a close look, you can see that there are two kinds of leaves: olive leaves, which symbolize peace, and oak leaves, which stand for eternity (because the oak is a very strong tree). The axe is justice, while the letters RF are the first initials of the words "French Republic," or as the French say: *La Republique Francaise.*

If you want to buy something in France, how do you pay for it?

Up until a few years ago, the French had their own currency, the franc. In 1999, the **franc** was replaced by the European currency named the **euro**.

The French Alps

The European Union (EU)

The European Union is a federation of 27 countries in Europe. Each is independent, but they all have some common characteristics, like their currency (money). If you visit Spain, Germany, or France, you will use the euro, even though each of these countries is independent and stands on its own.

This is the French franc.

And this is the euro.

The flag of the European Union

Did you know?

If the European Union were one big country (like the United States of America, which is made up of 50 states), it would be the third largest country in the world.

If you want to buy a souvenir in France, what currency will you use?

Answer: Euro, of course!

Once, many years ago...

Have you ever heard of the **French Revolution**? Or maybe the name Napoleon rings a bell? 😊 The history of France is fascinating.

People have lived in the area that is now called France as far back as the **Stone Age**. Back then it was not called "France," of course. As in all countries that have been in existence for many years, France was ruled throughout the ages by kings, **tyrants,** and sovereigns. But for over 130 years now, France has been headed by presidents. Let us try to put things in order so that we can understand France's history.

*A tyrant is an evil ruler.

In ancient times, the area where France is now was called **Gaul**, and it was inhabited by the Gallic tribes. Julius Caesar conquered Gaul and added it to the **Roman Empire**. In the sixth century, more than 1,400 years ago, Gaul was overrun by Germanic tribes called the "Franks." They were led by King Karl the Great, who conquered France as well as large areas of **Europe**. Although it was a powerful, vast empire, it did not last long. During the reign of **Karl the Great's** grandchildren, the empire was divided, and its **western part** became a separate kingdom, known today as **France.**

Through the years, many kings ruled the kingdom, but around 1000 AD, one **dynasty*** of kings came to power and ruled France for 800 years.

*Dynasty: a succession of rulers from the same family. The king's son is the heir to the king, and he becomes the king next. Then his son replaces him, and so on. Thus the kingship remains in the family.

Karl the Great

Did you know?
One of the most famous wars that took place during these years was the **Hundred Years' War** between France and England. You are probably guessing that it lasted 100 years... The truth is, it lasted 116 years (from 1337 until 1453)! 😊

Louis the 14th was a famous king who ruled France from 1661 until 1715. He was the most powerful and well-known king of all European monarchs, and you will read more about him later.

Have you ever heard about the French Revolution?

About 70 years after the reign of Louis the 14th, France was going through a difficult period. The kings who ruled the country were evil and dishonest. They imposed high taxes on the people, didn't care about their hardships, and prevented them from getting an education 😠. The kings seized people's lands, wasted money, and plunged France into a tough economic situation.

The situation became unbearable until the people united — the peasants, the educated people, and the workers — and fought against the rule of the kings. A war broke out in 1789, and that is what we call the **French Revolution**. It is an important event in the history of France and the world, because the common people succeeded in revolting and putting an end to the kingship. The kingdom was replaced by a republic — a form of government by the people.

King Louis the 14th

Did you know?
Many people in France were so poor that they could not even buy bread to eat, but the royalty did not care. It is said that the royal family was so removed from the common people that when Queen Marie Antoinette heard that the people had no bread, she responded, "Let them eat cake!"

The republican government did not last long and after a short period of chaos, Napoleon Bonaparte came to power (you will learn about him later) and declared himself emperor.

In 1814, France and Germany became bitter enemies and began to fight each other constantly. In 1914, the First World War broke out, and France joined the Allies who fought the Germans. France suffered many casualties, but thanks to the assistance of the American army, Germany was defeated.

The war cost much money, and France's economy fell into difficulty. The French people were hungry again.

During World War II, which broke out in 1939, France once again fought Germany, but the strong German army defeated the French and conquered large parts of France. The German occupation lasted about five years until 1944, when the **"Allied Forces"*** landed in Normandy in northern France. They freed the areas under German control, and France was once again reunited.

*The "Allied Forces" were a military force made up of soldiers from several countries who fought together against Germany.

At the end of the war, France invested heavily in creating work and financial stability and was slowly rehabilitated.

This is how soldiers once looked.

Famous leaders and rulers

Let us meet a few of the leaders and rulers who influenced France throughout the years:

Pleased to meet you — King Louis the 14th

King Louis the 14th lived from 1638 to 1715 and was one of the strongest monarchs in the history of France. He used to say, **"I am the state,"** because he thought he was the most **important** person in France — and the only one who had the authority to make decisions.

The father of Louis the 14th (King Louis the 13th, of course 😜), died prematurely, and young Prince Louis was crowned King at the age of five! His mother, Queen Anne, **replaced** him until he grew up and was old enough to sit on the throne.

Louis the 14th was a very **smart king**. He built his palace in Versailles (and not in the capital, Paris), and by doing so, he succeeded in removing those who tried to weaken him and take over the kingship. He spent the first part of his reign **fighting** his neighbors — Holland, Belgium, and Germany. A succession of impressive **victories** helped him strengthen and establish France as a leading country in Europe. But the final years of his reign were difficult and unpleasant for the French people. King Louis conquered Spain, but the cost of the war was high and its **large expenses** led France to an **economic crisis.**

Nevertheless, in the history of France, King Louis the 14th is regarded as a prominent and powerful monarch.

Among his impressive achievements are the building of the **Palace of Versailles** — which is considered the finest example of architecture and art in France — and the design of gardens and furniture that still bear his name: "Louis the 14th" style.

King Louis the 14th

Pleased to meet you — Napoleon Bonaparte

Napoleon Bonaparte was France's most significant ruler in the 19th century, and his influence spread all over Europe.

Did you know?
It is thought that Napoleon was a **short** man, but this is not true. The mistake is a result of the difference between the French measurement system and the English one. At his death, Napoleon was slightly **taller** than 5 French feet. The French "foot" was longer than the English one, so Napoleon was actually about 1.68 meters (or about 5 feet, 6 inches) tall, which was not considered so short in his time.

Napoleon was a brilliant military commander, known all over Europe for his great victories and many conquests. He was only **24 years old** when he was appointed general and commanded the French army. He was famous for his ability to build a **war strategy** that led to victories nobody thought were possible.

At the age of 35, Napoleon became the **ruler of France** after the turbulent times of the French Revolution. He succeeded in stabilizing the country and taking care of its citizens. A year and a half after being made the Emperor of the French, he was also crowned King of Italy.

Did you know?
During that period, the Pope crowned the emperors, to symbolize that the emperor was subject to the Church and the Pope. During Napoleon's coronation as Emperor of the French, however, he took the crown from the Pope and placed it on his own head — as if to say that he, Napoleon, did not wish to be lesser than anyone!

Napoleon Bonaparte

Napoleon married **Josephine de Beauharnais,** but they were divorced 13 years later. (It is said the reason was that Josephine couldn't have children.) Napoleon then married **Marie-Louise of Austria**, daughter of the Emperor of Austria, possibly in order to unite the two nations.

Despite his impressive achievements, Napoleon's end was tragic. His army suffered a great loss in a war against Russia. Out of 500,000 soldiers who went to war, less than 100,000 survived, and Napoleon returned to Paris defeated and humiliated. Napoleon's position became unstable, and a group of allied countries united in order to defeat the French army. They conquered Paris, forced Napoleon to leave his office, and sent him away to exile on the isle of Elba.

A short while later, Napoleon tried to recruit an army of volunteers in order to fight and get back his position as emperor. The famous Battle of Waterloo was Napoleon's last battle, and he was beaten by the English army. He was driven away from France and exiled to the island of St. Helena, where he spent the rest of his life. **Napoleon died before his 52nd birthday.**

Napoleon left an impressive legacy: imposing **architectural structures** (such as the Arch of Triumph — which you will read about later), and a code of advanced laws that did not exist until his time. These included the **Equality Laws,** which state that all human beings are born equal and all have a right to acquire property.

Napoleon is also remembered for his brilliant quotes.* Here are some of them:

"An army marches on its stomach."

"You are longer than me, not taller." (This was his answer to a soldier who claimed to be taller than Napoleon.)

"If you want a thing done well, do it yourself."

"You can do everything with a spear, except sit on it."

*"Quote" means to repeat words or sentences that someone else said.

Pleased to meet you — Charles de Gaulle

Charles de Gaulle was **one of the greatest politicians of the 20th century**. He was born in 1890 and died 80 years later. De Gaulle was a young and gifted officer. He was known for his ability to thwart German military tactics during **World War II, when Germany** was trying to invade France and other parts of Europe. Following the German invasion of France, de Gaulle escaped to England and was appointed Prime Minister in Exile (a prime minister who runs his country from another place). In 1944, de Gaulle entered Paris at the head of the **Allied Forces,** liberated the city from the Germans, and became famous all over the world.

In the late 1940s, de Gaulle opposed the way France was run and retired from military and political life. However, in 1958 he was called back to **head the country** when times were difficult economically and politically. During his period as **president**, de Gaulle strengthened France's economy and its position in the world, and made France a powerful, independent country.

Did you know?
About **75 million** visitors go to France annually, much more than the number of tourists who visit Spain or the United States, for example.

Who am I?

Quizzes!

- Although I was considered a short man, I am the most famous military figure in the history of France.

- Despite the fact that France suffered economic hardships during my time, I am regarded as its most successful king.

- Thanks to me, France today is a modern and powerful state.

Answers: (1) Napoleon; (2) Louis the 14th; (3) De Gaulle

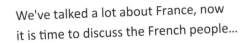

We've talked a lot about France, now it is time to discuss the French people...

Culture and customs

Do you know any French people? Have you ever heard the names Jean-Paul, Pierre, Jacques, or Marie-Louise? We've talked a lot about France, but what about the French people?

What is unique about the French? What do they like to do in their **spare time?** Where do they work? Which **customs are unique** to France?

● The French appreciate food and like to talk about it. They not only enjoy cooking and buying good food, but they also arrange the food on the plate in a special, fine way (a chapter will be dedicated to French food).

● The French are aesthetic people. Their well-planned streets and avenues, their lovely gardens, their excellent taste in fashion, and their food markets — which sometimes look like food museums — make it is easy to understand the French admiration for beauty and aesthetics.*

*Aesthetics: a branch of philosophy dealing with the criticism of art, the nature of beauty, and the awareness of it.

● Their patriotism: You may have noticed that the French love their culture, especially their language. It seems as if they don't even make an effort to speak or understand other languages. Most of the signs, the menus in the restaurants, and the tourism booklets are written in French only. Even foreign TV programs — and not only those for children — are dubbed* into French!

*Dub: to record voices over the actors' voices in a film put the film's dialogue in a different language.

What impression did the French make on you?

1. They are charming.

      2. They are quite nice.

   3. Not so nice...

      4. I cannot make up my mind.

Bon appétit! — French cuisine (cooking)

The French are known for their **excellent, tasty dishes.** Most adults will tell you that the French style of cooking is superb (they may use other descriptions, but they all agree that the cuisine is excellent 😉).

The French love to eat. They may not eat large quantities of food, but they love to **buy** it, **prepare** it, and **talk** about it.

You cannot go to France without knowing certain basic and important facts about French food. Leonardo will give you some idea about what is going on:

Where to eat

● A patisserie
— a bakery with sweet cakes and pastries. The shop windows of the patisseries are so beautiful and yummy that you may want to take their picture. Why not?

Paste a souvenir picture of a patisserie's shop window here.

Cremerie — a store for cheese

● **Boulangerie** — a shop for bread and cakes. Some of these shops bake their own pastries in a bakery at the back of the store, and the smell that comes from them is wonderful.

● **Cremerie** — a store for cheese. For those of you who like cheese, this is heaven...

● **Café** — when you say "café" in French, it means a coffee shop. Most cafés serve light lunches as well.

● **Brasserie** — a large restaurant serving local food and alcoholic beverages.

● **Bistro** — a small restaurant serving simple meals in a homey setting.

● **Food markets** — there are several food markets in France and visiting them is a wonderful experience — the smells, the colors, and the variety of groceries are delightful.

Now that we've learned about the places where you can eat, let's get to know some of the tasty dishes you should eat when in France. When you sit in a restaurant and look at the menu, or stand in line at a patisserie, take a look at the list below and find these recommended dishes:

Pastries

If you don't like to try new foods (meat or side dishes), ask your parents to order a tasty sandwich. Paris is a paradise for bread lovers. If you like anything made of dough and baked in an oven, then try these: brioche (a kind of light-textured bread), an éclair (pastry filled with cream and covered in chocolate), or a croissant, of course.

Cheese

France is famous for its variety of **cheese**. It is recommended to taste Camembert, Pont l'Éyvêque and chevre (goat cheese). The French sour cream, called "crème fraiche," is very tasty.

Meat

If you wish to order chicken, look for the word *poulet* in the menu. If you want veal, look for *veau*.

And what about desserts?

The names of traditional French desserts are enough to make your mouth water:

- Tart Tatin (an upside-down apple pie)
- Profiterole (a small, round cream puff served with ice cream and hot chocolate sauce)
- Flan (baked custard — a sort of pudding)
- Crème Brulee (custard topped with a layer of hard caramel)

And how can we do without...
a chocolate mousse!

Pastries

Leonardo has just landed in France, and he already has the urge to try some delicious foods. Help him find them...

Where can he find some good cheese? _____

Where can he find tasty bread? _____

And if he wants something sweet to eat, where would you advise him to go? _____

Answers: A cremerie; A boulangerie; A pâtisserie

What new dishes did you see?
More importantly, what new dishes did you taste?

Name of the dish (if you don't know its name, write down what it looks like)	Did you taste it? (yes or no)	Description of dish (what does it include; how does it look)	How do you grade it? (bad, good, or excellent)

Did you taste a dish that looks exactly like something you eat at home, but tastes different?

_____

_____

Majority rules! A family vote:

Which dish was voted as favorite among your family members?

Name	What dish did you like the best?

The winning dish is: _____

How do you say it in French...?
(a handy dictionary)

It is easy to recognize the French language. When you hear it, you know right away what it is. Some French words sound almost the same in English (for example, "dinner" in English and *le dinner* in French) because both languages were derived from Latin.

Do you want to feel a little independent and speak some French?
Here are some words that will help you. You can practice them later on...

Being polite

Hello/good morning	Bonjour
Good evening	Bonsoir
Bye-bye/see you	Au revoir
Yes	Oui
No	Non
Please	S'il vous plait
Thank you	Merci
Thank you very much	Merci beaucoup
You're welcome	De rien
Excuse me	Excusez moi
Sorry/pardon me	Pardon
I do not speak French.	Je ne parle pas Francais.
Do you speak English?	Parlez vous Anglais?

At the restaurant

Restaurant	
Breakfast	Restaurant
Lunch	Le petit dejeuner
Dinner	Le dejeuner
Butter	Le dinner
Bread	Du beurre
A cup	Du pain
A glass	Une tasse
Fork	Un verre
Knife	Une fourchette
Spoon	Un couteau
Sugar	Une cuillere
Wine	Du sucre
Salt	Du vin
Pepper	Du sel
Croissants	Du poivre
Honey	Des croissants
Eggs	Du miel
An omelette	Des oeufs
Snails	Une omelette
Sausage	Des escargots
Salad	Du saucisson
Soup	Une salade
Fish	Une soup
Meat	Du poisson
Beef	La viande
Lamb	Le boeuf
Pork	Le mouton
Steak	Le pork
Veal	Le steak
Chicken	Le veau
Noodles	Le poulet
Pasta	Les nouilles
Potatoes	Les pates
Cheese	Les pommes de terre
The bill	Du fromage
	La note

Competition!

Who remembers more French words?

Ask each other and award points for each correctly remembered word.

Who won?

Need to buy something?

One	Un
Two	Deux
Three	Trois
Four	Quatre
Five	Cinq
Six	Six
Seven	Sept
Eight	Huit
Nine	Neuf
Ten	Dix
One hundred	Cent
One thousand	Mille

Practice a few sentences to help you memorize the words:

● In English — Excuse me, I don't speak French.

In French — Excusez moi je ne parle pas Francais.

● In English — How much is a ticket to the subway (the Metro)?

In French — _____

● In English — Good evening, where is the train station?

In French — _____

● Say your home phone number in French.

● Count from 1 to 10 in French.

● Say your hotel room number in French.

What do you know about France?

1. In what continent is France located?

2. True or false? France is the third largest country in Europe.

3. Which natural border separates France, Italy, and Switzerland?

4. True or false? The French Alps is the name of a river.

5. What is the French flag called?

6. What colors appear on the French flag?

7. What currency is used in France?

8. True or false? The Arch of Triumph was built by King Louis the 14th.

9. Complete: "If they don't have bread let them eat..."

10. True or false? Napoleon met his death while fighting in a battle for the glory of France.

11. Which famous French king was crowned at the age of five?

12. True or false? Charles de Gaulle was the king who built the Versailles Palace.

13. Who built the Versailles Palace?

14. What is a patisserie?

15. How do you pronounce "croissant"?

16. What is Tart Tatin?

17. How do you say "good morning" in French?

Answers on page 67.

Paris
Here we come!

Before you start reading about Paris...

What do you already know about this city?

_____

_____

_____

What are you most hoping to see and do in Paris?

_____

_____

_____

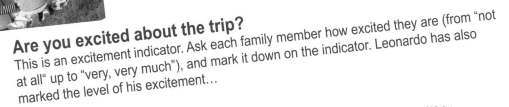

Are you excited about the trip?

This is an excitement indicator. Ask each family member how excited they are (from "not at all" up to "very, very much"), and mark it down on the indicator. Leonardo has also marked the level of his excitement...

not at all   very,
                                                    very much

Leonardo

Welcome to PARIS

Paris, the capital of France, **is one of the most beautiful cities in the world,** if not the most beautiful of them all. If this is your first visit to Paris, you should know that it is situated on the **river Seine** and among its attractions are special **streetlights**, picture-like **gardens**, **impressive buildings**, famous cathedrals and museums, and excellent food!

Take a look around you: isn't it a beautiful city?

Did you know?
Paris is called "The City of Light."
Can you guess why?

Where did Paris get its name?

People lived in Paris as far back as 2,300 years ago (third century BC). About 1,500 years ago, it was named "Paris" by the King of the Franks, after the Parisii tribe who lived there at the time.

One of the most important people to leave his impact on Paris and the way it looks today was **Baron Haussmann**, who lived between 1809 and 1891. Paris was once **a small, crowded** town with no housing for the many people who settled there. Baron Haussmann started planning reforms: narrow streets became broad avenues, new buildings were built, and a system of underground railways was constructed. A system of sewers was dug and expansive gardens were laid out. Thanks to the Baron, Paris is such a beautiful city.

Did you know?
Paris is one of the most crowded cities in Europe. About 25,000 people live on each square kilometer (or less than half a square mile).

What does Paris look like?

Here is a map of the city.

If you take a close look, you can see that Paris is divided into sections and each section has a number. These sections are called **"arrondissements."** The center of the city is arrondissement number one.

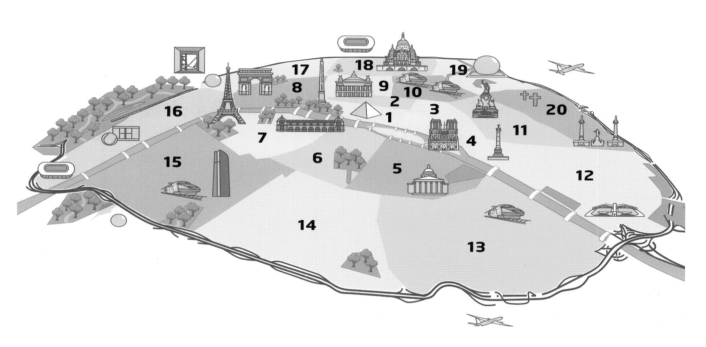

In which arrondissement are these monuments located?

Notre-Dame ——————————

Montasier Park ——————————

Arch of Triumph ——————————

Champs-Elysees ——————————

Eiffel Tower ——————————

The Louvre ——————————

Answers on page 66.

Things you see only in Paris

Paris is a very special city, and there are things you can find only there.

Wallace fountains

Take a good look around you: at the streets, the gardens, the buildings. Sniff the air, look at the stores. **Do you see some other things that make Paris special?** Write them down so you won't forget.

_____

_____

_____

_____

billboards

Did you notice the drinking fountains scattered throughout Paris?
These public drinking fountains are called **Wallace fountains** because they were a gift to the city from a rich Englishman named Sir Richard Wallace. He donated 50 fountains to the city 😮.

Transportation in Paris

There are several ways to get from one place to another in Paris. Here is some information, so you too will feel confident:

The first and fastest way is to use the Metro.
The French say that there is no place in Paris more than a five minutes' walk from a Metro station. This means you will not walk more than five minutes before you come across a Metro station, which will take you wherever you wish to go. This is very convenient.

Can you figure out what the main disadvantage of using the Metro is for tourists?

Did you know?
There are about 300 Metro stations in Paris.

This is the sign of the Paris **Metro** – whenever you see the letter "M" (it's not McDonald's...), you'll know there is a Metro station close by.

The second and more interesting way is by bus.
A bus can take you almost anywhere in Paris. The biggest advantage of traveling by bus is that you can see the city during the ride, meet other tourists, and take pictures as well (if the bus is slow and you are fast enough).

What do you think is the main disadvantage of traveling by bus?

The third and most expensive way is by taxi.
The biggest advantage of traveling by taxi is being driven to your exact destination; there is no need to decipher a map or remember where to get off. If the driver happens to be nice, he will tell you about the places you pass by or at least answer your questions (for example, where is the best delicatessen in the area...), assuming you speak French, of course.

What do you think is the greatest disadvantage of traveling by taxi?

The fourth, and most common way among tourists, is an open-bus tour.
Red double-decker buses travel all over Paris and pass by the city's famous historical places of interest. You can get off along the way, and later get back on. Travel by these buses is recommended for tourists who come to Paris for a short stay and want to see as many attractions as possible. Sit on the upper deck and you'll get a lovely view of the city from above.

What is the biggest disadvantage of taking a tourist bus?

There is SO much to see in Paris — where to begin?

Museums, cathedrals, **beautiful gardens,** and of course, Disneyland Paris — there are plenty of attractions in Paris. You only have to choose! Now it's time for Leonardo to lend a hand — he has gathered information about the most recommended sites and activities.

Tip!

Plan the route of the tour with your family. Whichever way you choose, you can use a bookmark to find each site when you reach it.

In Paris:
Champs-Elysees

Ask anyone which is the most famous avenue in Paris, and the answer will always be — the Champs-Elysees! The Champs-Elysees is one of the central avenues in Paris, and one of its symbols known all over the world.

Champs-Elysees Avenue is **three kilometers (or almost one mile) long**. In its upper part, there are gardens and palaces, among them the lovely Elysees Palace. In the lower part, there are prestigious **shops** and office buildings.

 Tip!

The oldest puppet show theater in Paris is located on the Champs-Elysees. It was founded about 200 years ago and is called Guignol (pronounced Gee-nyawl). It is highly recommended that you buy tickets to one of the shows. It is a wonderful experience!

A map of the street –

When you take a walk along the avenue, mark the places you see on this map (beautiful stores you like, impressive buildings, and such).

Concorde Square

Disney Store

Arch of Triumph

The Champs-Elysees

My impressions of the Champs-Elysees:

Which is the most beautiful store?

Which is the largest store?

Did we buy anything? If so, what?

L'Arc de Triomphe (the Arch of Triumph)

The Arc de Triomphe is a monument built by Napoleon in honor of his army, to commemorate the victory in the Battle of Austerlitz (where Napoleon's army beat the Russian and Austrian armies). The building of the Arch lasted 30 years, and unfortunately, Napoleon did not make it to the inauguration parade.

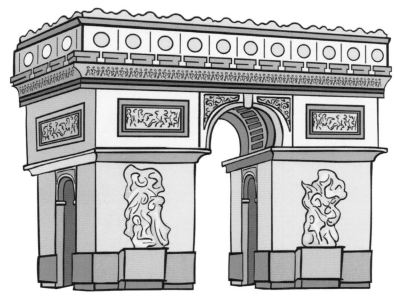

Did you know?
In order to finance the building of the Arc de Triomphe, Napoleon imposed a tax on the French citizens, making them donate 10 percent of their income.

The names of soldiers and officers killed in battle, and the names of the major battles of the Napoleonic Wars, are inscribed on the walls of the monument. The battles he lost are not mentioned on the Arch... ☺

It doesn't matter from which direction you approach the Arch, the closer you get, the bigger and more **impressive it looks**. When you stand underneath, it appears

enormous!

Tip!

Climb to the upper part of the Arch. It is 45 meters (or almost 148 feet) high, and the view from the top is marvelous.

Did you know?

The building of the Arch took a long time and when Napoleon's troops entered Paris, only the laying of the foundation was completed. A creative solution was found: a mock-up of the Arch, made of wood and cloth, was erected and decorated for the victory parade.

The Arc de Triomphe stands in the center of the Place Charles de Gaulle (read about him later on), formerly named Place de l'Etoile, which means "star" in French. There are 12 avenues diverging from the square (in memory of Napoleon's 12 victorious battles), reminding one of a **star**.

Arc de Triomphe

Help Leonardo to find the street names. Write each name in order, in its proper place.

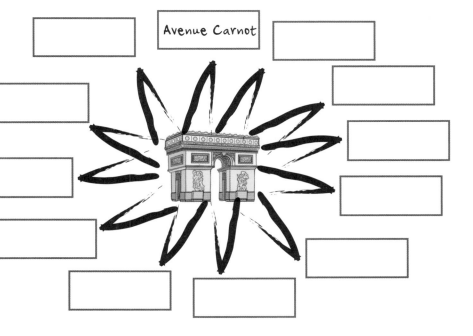

Avenue Carnot

Answers on page 66.

The Eiffel Tower

The Eiffel Tower is one of the most famous towers in the world. In 1887, the French were looking for a **structure** to mark the centennial (100 years) celebration of the French Revolution. One hundred architects and engineers sent their proposals, detailing how the structure should look.

Gustave Eiffel was an engineer who specialized in the planning and building of enormous bridges, which were unusual back then. He suggested erecting a huge metal tower. The Eiffel Tower opened to the public exactly **100 years after the French Revolution**. About five million people visit the Tower each year.

Eiffel Tower

Quizzes!

How tall is the Eiffel Tower?

a. 5 meters (16-1/3 feet)
b. 30 meters (98-1/2 feet)
c. 324 meters (1,063 feet)
d. 1 kilometer (3,281 feet)

 Tip!

If you are interested in the history of the Tower and would like to know how it is painted and kept clean, watch the film that is screened on the first level of the Tower.

Answer: C - 324 meters (1,063 feet)

Third level
height

Second level
height

First level
height

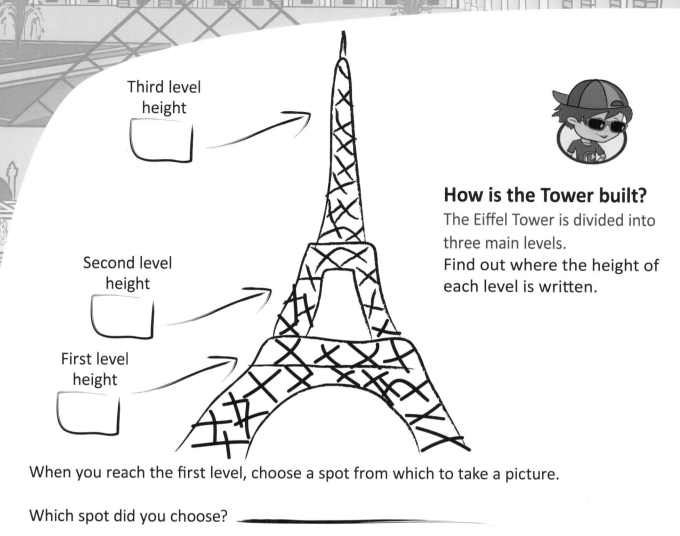

How is the Tower built?

The Eiffel Tower is divided into three main levels.
Find out where the height of each level is written.

When you reach the first level, choose a spot from which to take a picture.

Which spot did you choose? _____

Can you find the same spot on each level and photograph it from different heights?

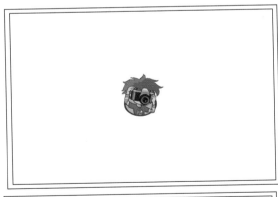

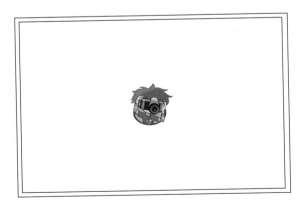

Answers:
1. 57 meters (187 feet)
2. 115 meters (377-1/4 feet)
3. 276 meters (905-1/2 feet)

45

To reach the top of the Tower, you must climb 1,652 stairs 😮.
Even if you are willing to face the challenge, it is impossible:
tourists can climb the stairs up to the second level
only, and from there upwards, there's an elevator 🙂.

A few things not everyone knows about the Eiffel Tower:

- The height of the Tower changes between summer and winter by 15 centimeters (about 6 inches). The metals it is made of shrink and expand according to the weather: when it is cold, the metal shrinks — and when hot, it expands.

- When a strong wind blows, the Tower swings from side to side, 12 centimeters (4-3/4 inches) in each direction.

- They used 2.5 million rivets to build the Tower.

- Up **until 1930**, it was the **tallest structure** in the world.

- Five hundred people are employed in the Tower: 250 in maintenance, and 250 in the restaurants, the police station, and the post office.

- About 16,000 people visit the Tower every day!

Did you know?
About 100 years ago, the Tower was going to be dismantled. But there was a need for a tall structure to be used as an antenna for communication purposes, and luckily, it was allowed to remain. It's hard to imagine Paris without the Eiffel Tower!

Centre Pompidou (the Pompidou Center)

The Pompidou Center is actually a **huge museum** of modern art.*
But there is still a lot to see and do in the Centre Pompidou, even if you
don't visit the museum itself to see paintings and works of art.

Should we go there?

Yes! For several reasons: First and foremost, the building itself is completely
different from any building you've seen so far in Paris. **It looks as if it were
built by children from Lego blocks** and colorful pipes.
Street performers, jugglers, and mime artists perform in the plaza in front
of the museum. It's **fun** to sit on one of the benches or wander among the
performances. It's a free show! Another reason to go is the escalator. It's true
that most kids have gone up and down escalators, but have you ever used an
escalator outside a building?

*If you are interested in finding out more about abstract art
and what can be found in museums, you can buy our special
Kids' Travel Guide — Paris Museums.

What is inside the building?

We will let you discover this by yourselves...

A hint: much more than works of art!

When you enter the building and walk around, write down what you see. (We will help you a little...)

We've already said that this building is different from what you've seen so far. When Georges Pompidou, who was the President of France at the beginning of the 1970s, decided to construct an art center (bearing his name, of course 😉), a design competition was held and more than 600 architects presented some very strange plans.

It seems that Pompidou was a very daring president, given that this is the plan he chose... 🙂 At first, many French people were angry when they saw the building, and some even ridiculed it.

What do YOU think of the building?

amazing	funny	ridiculous	beautiful	unique	ugly
☐	☐	☐	☐	☐	☐

The architects who planned the Center decided that instead of hiding the electric, water, and air-conditioning systems, they would emphasize them and use them as decoration. Each color represents a different system:

The blue pipes are the air-conditioning system.
The green pipes are the water system.
The yellow pipes are for electricity.
The red pipes indicate the location of the stairs and elevators.
The white pipes are the ventilation pipes of the underground tunnels.

What other artists did you see or activities did you do? Write them here.

Stravinsky Square

Have you ever seen so many pretty, different-looking fountains?
Although this square is named after the famous composer **Igor Stravinsky**, these beautiful fountains were made by the sculptors **Jean Tinguely** and his wife, **Niki de Saint Phalle.**

Here you can see the pool at the Stravinsky Square without the fountains....
Write the number of each fountain in the right space in the pool.

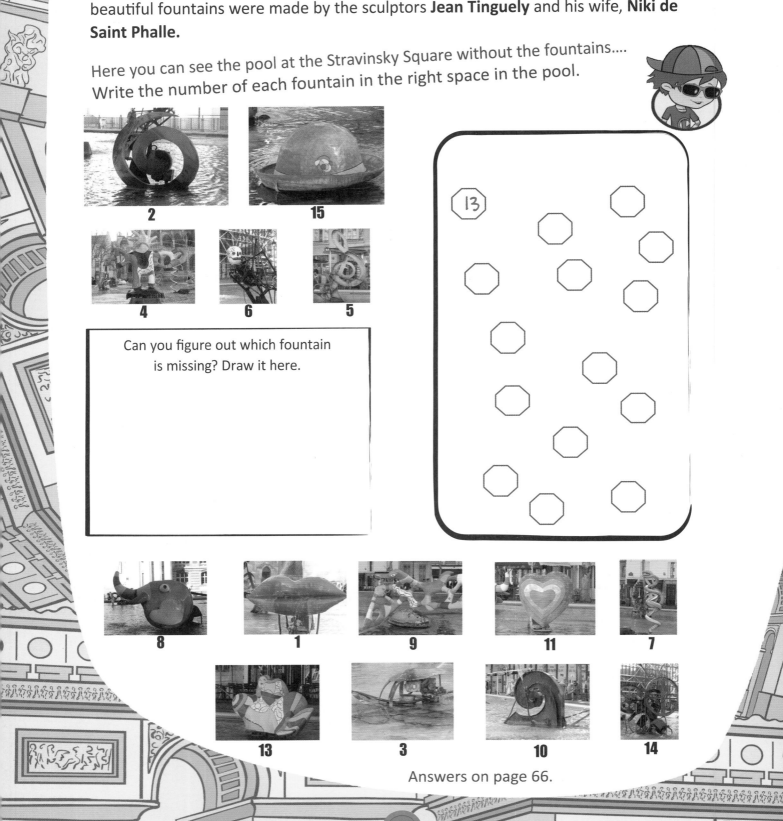

Can you figure out which fountain is missing? Draw it here.

2   15   4   6   5   13

8   1   9   11   7

13   3   10   14

Answers on page 66.

Notre-Dame Cathedral

Notre-Dame Cathedral is one of the most famous churches in Europe. It took 167 years to build the cathedral 😮. During the building, kings and rulers came and went, and each one **introduced changes** according to his tastes and to the style of the time.

The original cathedral was built of **wood**, and was completed in 1345, more than 662 years ago. Since then the building has been **remodeled** so many times that almost none of the original parts remain.

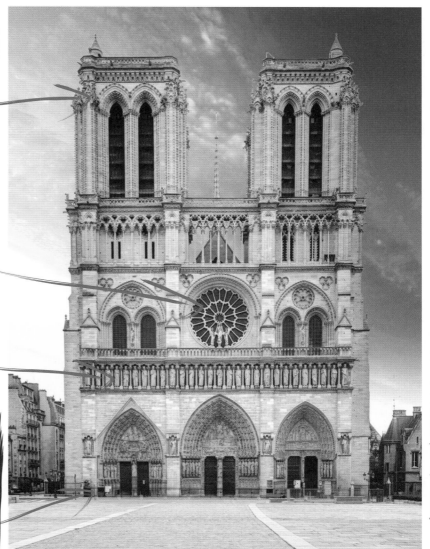

The South Tower –
Here are the famous bells from which Quasimodo swung in the book and movie *The Hunchback of Notre-Dame.*

The Rosette –
This was built more than 700 years ago. On either side of the circle are statues of Adam and Eve.

Kings Gallery –
The 28 statutes of kings of Israel and Judah are displayed here.

Three Gates –
They present themes from the world of Christianity. The central gate is dedicated to Jesus. The right gate shows Christian figures, and the left has Jewish figures.

Try to guess the diameter of the Rosette (the big circle in the middle).

Answer: 9 meters (29-1/2 feet)

How can Leonardo recommend you visit the cathedral without mentioning the book *The Hunchback of Notre-Dame*? The book was written by the famous French author **Victor Hugo,** and it tells about Quasimodo, the deaf hunchback who rings the bells of the cathedral and falls in love with Esmerelda, the beautiful gypsy. The book became more famous when Walt Disney Studios turned it into a wonderful movie. Leonardo strongly recommends that you read the book when you return home, or at least watch the movie. (It is possible, of course, to read the book **and** to see the movie 😊).

Did you know?

A few things that not everyone knows about Notre-Dame Cathedral.

- During World War I the French were afraid that the bombing would damage the cathedral and destroy the **ancient windows**. They therefore removed all the windows and stored them in a safe place. When the war ended all the windows were returned to their places.
- There is a giant pipe organ in the cathedral containing 7,800 pipes (900 are original). In 1992 a special program was initiated to **computerize the organ** and to connect it to the local communications network. The position of organist at Notre-Dame is considered to be one of the most desirable jobs in France.
- Until the Eiffel Tower was built, the Cathedral was the **highest spot** in Paris.

 Tiles with the names of streets and sites in Paris inscribed on them are embedded along the square in front of Notre-Dame. Find the tiles in the pictures. Mark each of the pictures above with a ✔ when you find the tile in the square.

La Defense

From far away you can see that the **La Defense** area is unique in Paris. The whole area is built of glass and concrete and looks a little like it doesn't belong to the local scenery.

The meaning of La Defense is "The Defense." Just like the Arch of Triumph, it was built in honor of the French army. (Do you remember which leader built the Arch of Triumph? That's right — Napoleon!) La Defense was also built as a huge arch, this time in modern style. The arch was built in honor of fraternity, which means "brotherhood," and is one of the three symbols of the French Revolution: **FREEDOM, EQUALITY, FRATERNITY**. The arch was dedicated at a special ceremony, marking the 200-year anniversary of the French Revolution.

The arch is **35 stories high** and you can take an elevator to the roof.

Go up on the roof and look southeast (you can easily spot the direction if you look for a long boulevard full of cars). What do you see from up there? Check off the sites that you see with a checkmark, and the sites you don't see with an X.

☐ The Seine River
☐ The Louvre
☐ Charles de Gaulle Airport
☐ Champs-Elysees
☐ EuroDisney
☐ Tuileries Gardens
☐ Parc de Villette
☐ The Picasso Museum
☐ The Arch of Triumph
☐ Notre-Dame Cathedral
☐ Concorde Square

IMMIGRATION OFFICER
✳ (4054) ✳
10 MAY 1999

And now write the names of the sites, from the closest (#1) to the farthest (#5).

1 _____
2 _____
3 _____
4 _____
5 _____

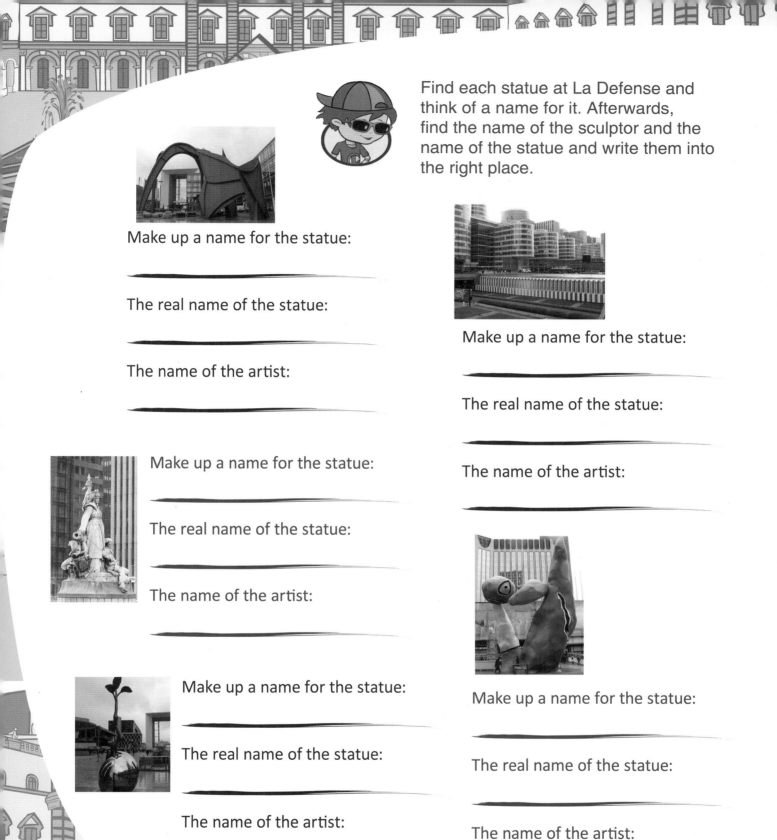

Find each statue at La Defense and think of a name for it. Afterwards, find the name of the sculptor and the name of the statue and write them into the right place.

Make up a name for the statue:

_____

The real name of the statue:

_____

The name of the artist:

_____

Make up a name for the statue:

_____

The real name of the statue:

_____

The name of the artist:

_____

Make up a name for the statue:

_____

The real name of the statue:

_____

The name of the artist:

_____

Make up a name for the statue:

_____

The real name of the statue:

_____

The name of the artist:

_____

Make up a name for the statue:

_____

The real name of the statue:

_____

The name of the artist:

_____

55

Tuileries Gardens

Welcome to the prettiest park in Paris.

In the past the park was closed to the common people, and only the royalty were allowed to visit. Luckily for us, now it is open to everyone, **and anyone who wants** can visit and enjoy a little nature in the middle of Paris.

Did you know?

Tuileries means "shingles." There are those who say that this is because there used to be a shingle factory in the park, and there are others who say that it is because of the special roof, made of **shingles**, on a palace that stood where the park is today. The palace burned down, and today there is a gallery called "Jeu de Paume" in its place.

Help Leonardo get from one end of the park to the other.

Besides the statues, you'll quickly find that the park can offer you lots of activities (especially if you are visiting in the summer), such as horseback riding and a puppet theater.

Triumphal Arch of Carousel

Does this arch look familiar? If so, you can probably guess who ordered it made.

That's right, it was Napoleon!

Stand **in front** of the arch and look around you. What do you see?

_____

What do you think of the Triumphal Arch of Carousel?

_____

Concorde Square

Concorde Square is one of the most famous squares in Paris. It took more than 10 years to build. At first it was called Louis the 15th Square, but since then it changed its name and we'll tell you why:

obelisk

This square has a **terrible story,** and there is not one French citizen who hasn't heard it. In his will, King Louis the 15th ordered that a square be built in his name. And so a square was built with a **fancy statue** of the king in the middle 😟.

Thirty years later the French Revolution broke out, and its leader decided to execute all the opponents of the revolution, using a guillotine. They changed the name to "**Revolution Square,**" took down the statue of the king, and in its place, put up a **guillotine.*** So it happened that the son of King **Louis the 15th** (called, of course, Louis the 16th), and his wife, Queen Marie Antoinette, were executed in this square. And they weren't alone: more than a thousand protesters were put to death in this square.

***What is a guillotine?** It is a device that was used for cutting off the heads of people who opposed the revolution.

The symbol of Concorde Square is the obelisk.

What is an obelisk? A type of monument that is tall and skinny with a point at the top.

The **obelisk** in Concorde Square is a present given to King Louis Philippe in 1829 from Muhammed Ali, the ruler of **Egypt**.

Yes, it is a very big and heavy gift 😉: it is 23 meters (75-1/2 feet) high and weighs 250 tons.

Did you know?
The real tip of the obelisk was stolen many years ago and never made it to France. The obelisk was capped with a golden tip instead.

And what about the symbols that are inscribed on the obelisk?

These drawings are called hieroglyphics — the writing system that the ancient Egyptians used. Although the obelisk was a present to the French, the hieroglyphics describe an Egyptian victory by King Ramses II. On the bottom, you'll find a description and drawings of how they managed to bring this giant thing from Egypt to France.

What is found around the obelisk?

_____

_____

Write down the appropriate number next to each part:
1 is the highest and 7 the lowest.

Can you remember the names of the sites that appear in the illustrations?

(A hint: You can use a map.)

1

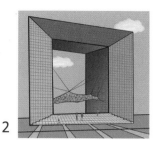

2

3

4

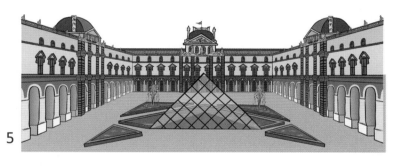

5

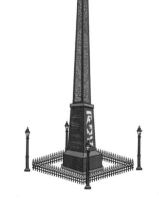

6

And to sum it all up...

Summary of the trip

We had great fun, what a pity it is over...

How long did we stay in Paris?

_____

At which hotel did we stay?

_____

What kinds of transportation did we use?

_____

Which sites did we visit?

_____

_____

Our most favorite place in Paris is: _____

The souvenirs we bought in Paris are: _____

The best food we ate in Paris was: _____

Grade the most beautiful places and the best experiences of your journey:

> **First place –**

> **Second place –**

> **Third place –**

Games and activites

Take turns and have each family member insert the words in one or two of the sentences. A funny story will come out!

Yesterday morning we drove to _____. We met _____ and _____.

We suggested they join us. They said _____ and went to _____.

When we neared ____, we saw the _____. We were really surprised. At first, we thought it was _____, but pretty soon we realized that it was _____. _____ said that the best thing would be to _____ and we all agreed.

When we reached the hotel, we decided to _____. Most of us thought it was a bad idea, but in the end, we all agreed. When we started walking towards _____, we found out _____.

That is why we have decided to drop the whole thing. We went back to _____ pretty tired but happy.

Solve the mystery of the three tourists...

Use the clues to figure out where the tourists are from, what they're wearing, and what they are doing on their vacation. Write the answers in the table:

- The three tourists arrived from Israel, America, and England.
- The tourist wearing the suit drinks tea.
- The tourist who drinks tea is not from America or Israel.
- The tourist with the pants and shirt didn't drink tea and didn't take any pictures today.
- The tourist from America is resting on the bench.
- The tourist who is taking pictures arrived on a night flight from Israel.
- The tourist from England is not wearing jeans and is not resting on the bench.

	What does he wear?	Where is he from?	What is he doing?
Tourist A			
Tourist B			
Tourist C			

Answers on page 67.

The words got lost...

Sort the words according to their numbers. Each set of numbers makes a sentence. Find the sentences and write them below:

4 the	2 France	7 the	1 what	8 Versailles	3 Paris	8 Palace	4 arch	5 Notre	1 fun	5 Dame
3 is	5 is	8 was	5 one	8 built	6 one	7 obelisk	8 by	2 is	8 king	7 is
6 of	1 we	4 of	2 located	6 the	7 the	5 of	4 triumph	3 also	8 Louis	5 the
5 most	3 called	8 the	5 famous	6 world's	4 commem-orates	3 the	8 14th	7 symbol	1 are	7 of
1 going	4 Napoleon's	2 in	6 biggest	3 city	7 the	4 army's	6 museums	5 cathedrals	3 of	1 to
2 Europe	5 in	6 is	7 Concorde	6 the	4 victory	7 Square	5 Europe	1 Paris	6 Louvre	3 light

1. _____

2. _____

3. _____

4. _____

5. _____

6. _____

7. _____

8. _____

Answers on page 67.

Coloring page

L'Arc de Triomphe (the Arch of Triumph)

Answers

Paris monuments (page 35)

Notre-Dame	4th arrondissement
Montasier Park	14th arrondissement
Arch of Triumph	Between the 16th and 17th arrondissements
Champs-Elysees	8th arrondissement
Eiffel Tower	Between the 7th and 15th arrondissements
The Louvre	1st arrondissement

The Arch of Triumph (page 43)

The names of the streets in Place de l'Etoile (Charles de Gaulle) in order:

1. Avenue Victor Hugo
2. Avenue Kleber
3. Avenue D'iena
4. Avenue Marceau
5. Avenue Des Champs Elysees
6. Avenue De Friedland
7. Avenue Hoche
8. Avenue De Wagram
9. Avenue Mac Mahon
10. Avenue Carnot
11. Avenue De La Grande Armee
12. Avenue Foch

Igor Stravinsky Square (page 50)

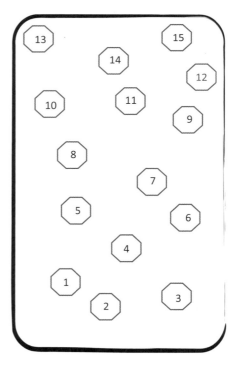

Trivia (page 32)

1. Europe
2. True (after Russia and Ukraine)
3. It's the name of French Alps
4. False—The name of a mountain range that separates France, Italy, and Switzerland
5. The Tricolor (for the three colors that appear on it)
6. Blue, white, and red
7. The euro
8. False—The Arch of Triumph was built by Napoleon to commemorate his big victories in battle.
9. Cake (attributed to Marie Antoinette)
10. False—He died on the island of St. Helena after he lost the Battle of Waterloo and was exiled from France.
11. King Louis the 14th
12. False—Charles de Gaulle was one of the strong people who helped to rebuild France and turn it into a great power.
13. King Louis the 14th
14. A pastry bakery
15. Krwas-son
16. A famous French dessert—sort of an upside-down apple pie
17. Bonjour

Who am I and what is my name (and what do I do...)? (page 63)

	What does he wear?	Where is he from?	What is he doing?
Tourist A	Jeans	Israel	Taking pictures
Tourist B	Pants and a shirt	America	Resting on the bench
Tourist C	A suit	England	Drink

Words got lost (page 64)

1. What fun — we are going to Paris.
2. France is located in Europe.
3. Paris is also called the City of Light.
4. The Arch of Triumph commemorates Napoleon's army's victory.
5. Notre-Dame is one of the most famous cathedrals in Europe.
6. One of the world's biggest museums is the Louvre.
7. The obelisk is the symbol of the Concorde Square.
8. Versailles Palace was built by King Louis the 14th.

A journal

Date

What did we do?

A journal

Date   What did we do?

A journal

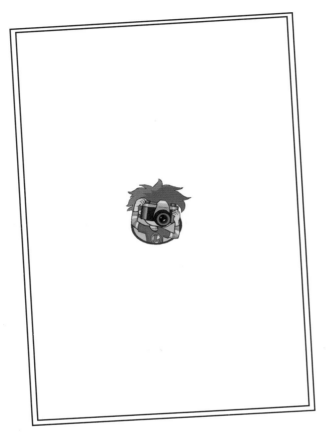

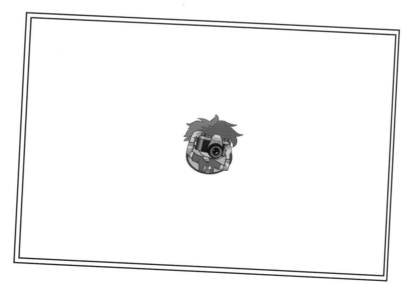

A journal

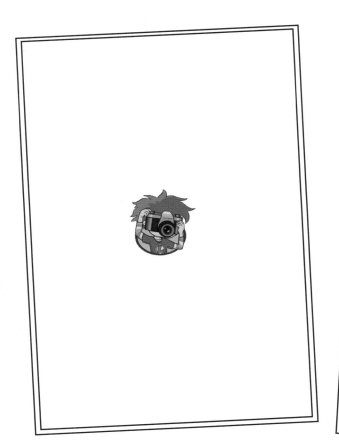

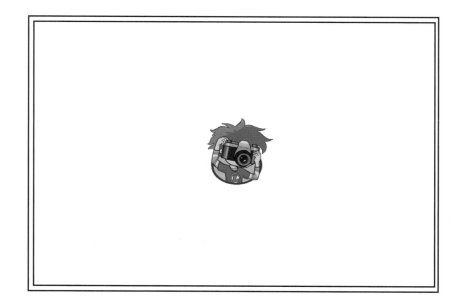

ENJOY MORE FUN ADVENTURES WITH LEONARDO AND FlyingKids

ITALY

THAILAND

JAPAN

FRANCE

GERMANY

SPAIN

AUSTRALIA

CHINA

USA

SPECIAL EDITIONS

UNITED KINGDOM

Kids' ACTIVITY BOOK SERIES

AGES 4-8

FOR FREE DOWNLOADS OF MORE ACTIVITIES, GO TO
WWW.THEFLYINGKIDS.COM